AF077214

HOW TO SURVIVE
IN THE CORPORATION

HOW TO SURVIVE IN THE CORPORATION
The Employee Handbook for Success

BOB JACK

How to Survive in the Corporation
Copyright © 2021 by Bob Jack.
All rights reserved.

No part of this publication may be reproduced, stored in a retrieval system or transmitted in any way by any means, electronic, mechanical, photocopy, recording or otherwise without the prior permission of the author except as provided by USA copyright law.

This novel is a work of fiction. Names, descriptions, entities, and incidents included in the story are products of the author's imagination. Any resemblance to actual persons, events, and entities is entirely coincidental.

The opinions expressed by the author are not necessarily those of URLink Print and Media.

1603 Capitol Ave., Suite 310 Cheyenne, Wyoming USA 82001
1-888-980-6523 | admin@urlinkpublishing.com

URLink Print and Media is committed to excellence in the publishing industry.

Book design copyright © 2021 by URLink Print and Media. All rights reserved.

Published in the United States of America

Library of Congress Control Number: 2021919487
ISBN 978-1-64753-970-2 (Paperback)
ISBN 978-1-64753-971-9 (Digital)

17.09.21

CONTENTS

Preface 9

Dedication 11

Introduction..13

How to survive in the corporation by taking
advantage of lucky brakes 15

How to survive in the corporation by learning
under a brilliant professional teacher 18

How to survive in the corporation by learning
the fundamental science, mechanical and
operating fundamentals of the business 21

How to survive in the corporation my having
a senior mentor in the organization 27

How to survive in the corporation when
senior management implements a policy that
is highly inequitable across the board to all
employees..31

How to survive in the corporation when
responsible for making a controversial
decision 36

How to survive in the corporation where it is
necessary to engage the support of an valued
subordinate and establish a solid working
relationship 40

How to survive in the corporation by dealing
with problem employees 43

How to survive in the corporation by
completing an important assignment on time
and within budget..46

How to survive in the corporation when
communicating directly with the CEO/
Chairman...49

How to survive in the corporation by
avoiding personal politics and focusing on
corporate steering mechanisms 52

How to survive in the corporation in the face
of the career setback 55

How to survive in the corporation when a
problem employee needs to be terminated..................59

How to survive in the corporation by researching the capabilities/capacity of your clients..62

Afterword..67

PREFACE

This book serves as an employee handbook which provides a roadmap for succeeding in the corporation environment. Millions of aspiring people serve in corporations throughout the country and abroad. Like people, corporations are individual creatures of organization, habits, and values. The corporation is considered a person under the law and like an individual is enshrined with dominant competencies in the form of personalities or cultures, abilities or resources and habits or structures. To choose the corporation is to choose a lifestyle that will last for many years - in many cases a lifelong commitment which will determine location for living, financial success, standard of living and time commitments throughout one's life. This book intends to equip the corporate person with some arrows in his or her quiver to help them navigate sometimes treacherous currents and challenges of corporate life.

DEDICATION

This book is dedicated to the memory of Ken E. Brunot. A powerful force in organizational leadership who in the late 1960s led the most successful and ambitious inner space program of the century in the deep sea drilling project at Scripps Institution of Oceanography. The deep-sea drilling project was a highly visible technological program involving the Glomar Challenger a drill ship that core sampled in record oceanic water depths up to 20,000 feet. Brunot's capacity to integrate highly diverse disciplines involving petroleum industry engineers with academic scientists was essential to the success of this legacy project which demonstrated the existence of continental drift, and rewrote geological textbooks throughout the world.

INTRODUCTION

After 40 years of existence in five different corporate cultures, each having its own structure and resources the only way to survive was to adapt my skills and learning to each different set of cultures, structures and resources. The technical and market characteristics in each industry markedly differed therefore adaptation of a given skill set was needed in each of these situations in order to survive. During the course of this career an array of experiences, problems, obstacles, and opportunities presented themselves and required careful navigation of the corporate waves that challenged me along the path to success. At 19 years old I encountered my first experience in the world of corporate existence. More of this will be covered in the chapters which follow. Each chapter is an individual experience which instructed on how to act, behave and respond to unique circumstances and challenges, and opportunities in the corporate environment. I learned that challenges can result in failure regardless of how hard you attempt to correct the situation, and I also learned lessons in which significant success was achieved and ultimately lifted me to career heights that were well worth the effort to learn. My corporate career journey started out as a mail boy at the age of 19 in an aerospace corporation and ended up in an executive position reporting directly to the president of a major environmental company in the engineering and construction management industry. By all measures it was a successful career in which the lessons I learned were invaluable and need to be captured and elucidated on in this book. I hope that this book will be a significant contribution to those people who take the time to read it and gain success from the lessons I learned.

How to survive in the corporation by taking advantage of lucky brakes

I had almost completed the first semester of my junior year at UCLA after having graduated from Citrus Community College with an associate of arts degree the semester before. It was 1960 and I was 19 years old the summer before launching into a new educational experience at UCLA. But my instincts for romance got the better of me and I proposed to my girlfriend and she accepted. There was no fundamental reason why I needed to get married I just reacted to the moment and proposed. After nearly completing my first Semester at UCLA I pulled up stakes from school where I was living in the dorm and moved back home to get ready for the impending marriage in December of 1960. It didn't take long for me to recognize the errors of my way and I immediately missed school and the possibility of playing on the UCLA baseball team. Nevertheless, I dug in and searched for a job and ended up landing a job as a mail boy at Aerojet General Corporation in Azusa, California. The supervisor assigned me to deliver telegrams and mail to Mahogany Row at Aerojet. That was a lucky break because I would be delivering to the top executives in the company and their secretaries. I did not realize this at the time but it turned out to be a very lucky break. The secretary to the treasurer to the company, Cathy Jensen, had taken a liking to me and an interest in what I wanted to do for a career. One day when delivering her mail she asked me what I wanted to do and I told her I wanted to be in Contracts and make that a career. The next day when I delivered her mail she told me to stop by the Director of Contracts office, also on Mahogany Row, and tell him of my interest. She had talked to him the day before about my interest so it was kind of a set up situation when I delivered his mail that day. Upon entering his office, I introduced myself. He was a big guy who had been a football player at Notre Dame I understood. He was very thoughtful. I told him of my interest in contracts. He picked up his phone and contacted my supervisor in the mail department and told him that I was putting in for a transfer, upon which he asked me if tomorrow was too soon to start my new job in contracts. I told him that would be fine and so he told my supervisor to make sure the transfer paperwork was effective the next day with a raise and a promotion. Therein launched my new career which over the next 40 years would net me a multi- million- dollar income. The next day I reported to work in contracts and started a new job. However, that was not the end of my luck. A few days later the manager of the contract department came to my office and told me he wanted me to accompany him to human resources where I would be presented with a scholarship to go back to school full-time. I was happy and stunned by my sudden lucky breaks. What I learned by this experience was that when luck presents itself that you can leverage it into either more luck or simply go on your way. In that job I learned the basics of contracts extremely well and it prepared me for a career which would last for 40 years. Therefore, when anybody has the chance to succeed because of luck take advantage of it immediately don't waste it. To this day Cathy Jensen is music to my ears and I will never forget her for taking an interest in me and setting up an opportunity to last for a lifetime.

How to survive in the corporation by learning under a brilliant professional teacher

It was 1963, age 22, and I had just graduated from California State University at Los Angeles. I was on my second interview after graduation. This Interview was for a job as a contract specialist at the architect- engineer division of Aerojet- General Corporation. The interview and the office were located in an old school building in Covina, California several miles from the corporate office of Aerojet -General Corporation. The interview was with the manager of contracts of the division by the name of Joe Eischen. Eischen was an intense individual wielding a flyswatter as he snapped at flies in his office during the interview. I had just graduated with high honors in economics with straight A's on my transcript, except for one B+. During the interview Joe said the reason he was interested in me was because of my grades in college. All of that studying made sense all of a sudden in talking with Joe. The interview went well. Joe made me an offer of

$550 a month (not bad for 1963) and I accepted. Shortly after reporting to work the first day I learned that Joe could be a mean and demanding boss who micromanaged and required a daily diary outlining what we were going to do for the day putting down times estimated for each task. These diaries had to be submitted by 9AM every morning. If Joe didn't like what he saw he would call us in and question as to what we were doing with our time. Joe was both an attorney and a CPA. He had worked hard for those degrees with his law degree being earned at night study. He was a brilliant contracts executive. Joe felt contracts had an important role to play on projects and if the project manager failed to perform he felt that the Contract Administrator should get directly involved in working out problems on the project. Joe had a reputation in the division for being a hard -nosed SOB. Nevertheless I could not have been trained by more intelligent individual who had a deep command of contracts and the law and federal procurement regulations. Joe's mark would remain on me for the rest of my career and I adopted many of the contracts principles which he had taught me during my two years in Contracts under his leadership. I remained at the architect engineering division of Aerojet for two years until I was recruited by Chevron under the liberal arts development program which had been chartered by the chairman of the board of the corporation. The purpose of the liberal arts development program at Chevron was to recruit and place high potential people into management positions where they could grow for the future. After leaving Aerojet and Joe Eischen, about a year later, I had dinner with Joe and we had a good discussion about my future career opportunities and about the past. That's the last time I saw Joe because shortly afterwards Joe passed away from a heart attack. Nevertheless Joe's legacy would live on in me for the rest of my career. I learned that it was invaluable to be trained by a highly qualified disciplined professional.

How to survive in the corporation by learning the fundamental science, mechanical and operating fundamentals of the business

It was 1965, age 24, and I have been recruited as a member by Chevron of its liberal arts development program. This program was the brainchild of the chairman of the board who believed from what he had witnessed within the company that there were not enough liberal arts graduates (business, economics, marketing, human resources) personnel within the organization in high level positions. Consequently, he chartered human resources at Chevron to develop a liberal arts development program which would recruit people both from within the company and outside who showed high potential for advancement in the Corporation, and that they be trained and developed to be equipped for high potential positions at Chevron (then known as Standard Oil Company of California). Consequently, and in order to advance in an upward direction, I left the aerospace company at Aerojet

General as a contract specialist, and accepted an offer to join Chevron's liberal arts development program. The program was designed by Lloyd Plank a senior human resources executive at Chevron. The program was developed around two principal phases. First there was a three month stint at corporate headquarters in San Francisco with the participants in the program being exposed to high level managers that represented the different functional disciplines within the corporation. That would include marketing, finance, production, refinery manufacturing and transportation. Chevron also had highly valued land assets around the world that were the subjects of development. During the three-month phase at corporate headquarters for the program the participants, approximately 10 persons, were exposed to high levels of senior management in the various disciplines that comprised Chevron. These managers would make presentations of the purpose and nature of the assets assigned to them in the various operational markets of Chevron – exploration, production, transportation, refinery, marketing and land development. The participants in the program were shuttled off to field sites where these operations were being conducted and given first-hand tours by the managers of the plants and assets of Chevron. Participants were given tests on what they had learned for purposes of evaluating their progress during the program, and interacting on a personal level among themselves in group sessions where they could develop a rapport and hash over details they had learned concerning the presentations and field visitations they had experienced. The second phase of the program was an assignment to one of the operating units of the company where they could learn the basic rudimentary discipline from hands-on experience. My initial assignment was in the producing department in Southern California at the division level. The first day I reported to work to a drilling supervisor by the name of Ken Brunot. Ken had a square chin and the rugged appearance and build of a football player. I reported that first morning in a suit and tie. The first thing Ken did was tell me to go home and put on my work clothes because I was going to be assigned to work as a rotary helper (roughneck) on a drilling rig. For the next two months I rotated shifts as a member of the rig in Whittier ,California where I worked on the drilling rig floor operating the tongs that gripped the drill pipe. I learned about drilling operations, the functions of drilling mud in the drilling process, how to operate the tongs that gripped the drill pipe and what the responsibilities of each member of the drill team happened to be. I also learned about logging and directional drilling including seismic activities essential to identifying oil reservoirs. These were fundamental aspects of the business that it was important to understand. I became friends with Ken who imparted a great deal of knowledge about the drilling operations.

Shortly after we met Ken e departed Chevron for Scripps Institution of Oceanography in La Jolla, California where he became the manager of the Deep Sea Drilling Project (DSDP) funded by the National Science Foundation (NSF). This project would become known as the top inner space program of the century. Nevertheless my days at Chevron had time yet to run, and the learning experience would grow in the next year as my assignments led to other activities in the drilling field and production activities. After my assignment on the drilling rig, I initiated activities as a field operator serving as a roustabout. In that capacity I learned how to take viscosity measurements, repairing oil field equipment including production operating equipment and serving as a general laborer in the oil field. All of this was invaluable in understanding the core technologies and operations of the oil business. After this assignment I was tasked to human resources in the producing department to formulate a drilling operators training program which I would then implement on the drilling rigs in the division. I introduced this training program as the trainer of new crews entering the drilling field within the company relying on my experience of two months on the rig. Following this project I was assigned to the Organization and Cost Control Department (O&CC) which was Chevron's version of an internal audit function designed to increase efficiencies and reduce costs in the organization. I performed several studies in this capacity. One of them was to examine the use of company owned automobiles throughout the division and determine if they were being efficiently utilized in an attempt to reduce costs. As a result of my study the automobile pool in the division was reduced and sizable costs were saved. Following this assignment, I received an evaluation of performance and given a sizable promotional increase. In this review my potential was rated as a Vice President in an operating unit—a good review I found the producing department to be a challenging, exciting and rewarding assignment and I had hoped for a permanent job in the operation. Nevertheless, the company felt that my ultimate potential was in a non-technical department because of my liberal arts background and I was given an assignment in the division land and legal operation. After an initial orientation of 1 to 2 months I was placed in charge of land and legal division administration reporting to the division manager. In this position I was in charge among other things of the production of land lease documents for the division that would ultimately be executed by landowners for royalty rights. I also assisted the division manager with salary administration for the entire division and for the administration of royalty payments to landowners within the company. This included the urban drilling operations and downtown Los Angeles oil plays including directional drilling from permanent buildings in production of oil reservoirs around the city. After about a year on the Land a Legal administration job an opportunity opened up through Ken Brunot who had been named manager of the deep sea drilling project at Scripps Institution of Oceanography in La Jolla, California. This was a National Science Foundation funded effort that was to become the inner space program of the century. I was offered a position as the director of contracts and procurement at a sizable increase in pay and accepted the job. This turned out to be a wonderful decision to be a key member of one of the most significant projects of the time, presented a challenging job opportunity and a large pay boost. The training and experience gained at Chevron in the fundamental operations, science and mechanics of the petroleum industry would serve me well as a member of the deep sea drilling project for a number of years to come. The lesson I learned was that becoming familiar with the fundamental operating science and mechanics of the business was an important learning experience that could be adapted to future opportunities to which I became involved. I transferred to Scripps institution of oceanography to be a member of the DSDP in 1967 at age 26. Due to good luck and hard work my career progress had been excellent and just getting started.

How to survive in the corporation my having a senior mentor in the organization

It was 1976 at the age of 35. After five years, I was ready to make a move up from my position as a senior Contract Administrator at General Atomic company in San Diego California. I was working as a senior member of the government contracts office at the company and I reported to the manager of contracts who was well situated in his job and showed no signs of moving out of it at any time in the near future. Consequently, I developed a résumé and sent it out to a number of companies and started to interview. One of the companies I interviewed was Southern California Edison in the contracts department. I was interviewing for a senior administrator in the contracts department. I had a salary expectation on the table that was a serious number and I was being paid well in my present job at General Atomic. I interviewed with the manager of contracts who I found to be a very professional individual and I liked him. We got along well in the interview but Southern California Edison unfortunately could not meet my salary expectations. This manager told me that he wanted to hire me but he understood he was not in a position to do so at the present time with the salary constraints that he faced. Instead he put in a personal word for me with Roy Gaunt, a vice president of the power division at Parsons in Pasadena, California who he knew to have a need for a Principal Contract Administrator at a higher salary level. As a consequence, I interviewed with the vice president at Parsons in the power division and was offered a principal contracts administrator position and a promotion at a higher salary as I had asked. The vice president who made me the offer was a sales vice president of the division. The manager of the power division was an empty slot which was to be recruited and filled by a senior Vice President from outside Parsons. It was soon announced that a senior executive from Braun Corporation in Alhambra would be transferring to Parsons to take over the position of SR VP of the power division. By coincidence the name of this Senior Vice President was Bill Jack. There was no relationship between us of a family nature but we both had the same last name and this was of great interest to the new senior Vice President Bill Jack. Shortly after joining Parsons he came to my office sat down with me and he said the first thing I want to know is "are we related?". We determined that we were not related in the family sense but we had the same last name and this was an interesting development because of the perception it created within the company. Bill and I became quickly attached in an organizational sense both being highly profit motivated and both believing in toughness in negotiations with clients. Bill was a no nonsense manager, an incredible talent. It was an honor to work for him and have found a new mentor at a senior level within Parsons. Bill Jack backed me up on decisions and supported me in my role with the company. Soon after Bill joined Parsons as a Senior VP of the Power Division, the Systems and Power divisions were merged into one single division named the Systems Division, which was a much larger division with global activities in Saudi Arabia and in the military market, it was also the principal construction manager for DOE's strategic petroleum reserve program in Louisiana and Texas. This opened up a significant opportunity for me since the systems division had a built-in Contract Department and shortly after the merger of the two divisions Bill Jack appointed me to be manager of the combined contracts operations for the division. There were many hardships to overcome after this appointment was made due to the fact that existing members of the system division contracts group felt they should've been selected for the new manager position of the contracts department. Nevertheless, Bill Jack appointed me and within a short period of time I set about two re-organize the contracts group and transfer half of the staff to another department along with their job charges since they were not performing actual Contract Administration activities, rather they were project accountants. I made sure that the department retained the most qualified people on staff and in a short period of time released or transferred those who were not highly qualified contract specialists. What was remaining was the cream of the crop of the contract personnel in the company (three of them were eventually promoted to a VP position). This built a future which would in several years see this contract group become the Parsons corporate contracts group, an organization that I would manage for several years until moving on to Parsons' environmental company. What I learned from this entire experience was that it helps immensely to have a senior level mentor in the company who is there to back you up and support you and promote you to more senior levels in the company. I will always be grateful to Bill Jack for being that mentor and friend.

How to survive in the corporation when senior management implements a policy that is highly inequitable across the board to all employees

In the late 1970s the global engineering and construction company Parsons initiated an Employee Stock Ownership Plan (ESOP) to which about 30% of the stock of the company would be allocated. ESOP is a defined contribution retirement plan which is managed by an ESOP trust which holds the stock that will be allocated to the accounts of employees on a periodic basis. This is an example of worker capitalism to the largest degree in which employees actually take beneficial ownership to the stock of their company. In this case Parsons had distributed about 30% of its stock to the ESOP trust, the other approximate 70% being held by public stockholders on the New York Stock Exchange. In 1984, for a number of strategic reasons, Parsons management including its CEO determined that a 100% ESOP owned company would be in the interests of both the company and the employees. Parsons engaged financial and legal experts to structure the internal and external parameters of this deal. Parsons' plan was to execute a tender offer for both the outstanding approximately 70% of publicly owned stock and for the close to the 30% owned by the existing ESOP trust. In establishing the internal structure Parsons, questioned by some, established executive reporting relationships in such a way that there was a possible conflict of interest between the executives serving as members of the two ESOP trusts and executives at the senior management level to whom the existing ESOP trustees of both new and existing ESOPS reported. The new existing ESOP trust tendered for the publicly held shares at $32 per share. The tender offer for the employee-owned shares of the predecessor ESOP amounted to only $28 per share thereby establishing a differential price for the stocks. This turned out to be a problem closing the deal, and the cause of it was that the company did not appear to have the financial capacity to pay $32 per share for all of the shares. This shortchanged the employee held shares by $4 a share under the pre-existing ESOP trust. My position at the time was manager of contracts reporting only three tiers down from the CEO. I was well-known in the company because of this position. When it became clear what the situation was and that the employees and the predecessor ESOP were being shorted by four dollars per share, I quickly assessed the conflicts of interest involved in the transaction and found them to be in my opinion a significant factor. The trustees of the predecessor trust were beholden to senior management for their compensation, and employment and in a weak position to negotiate a $32 per share value. I was displeased with the outcome and knew it was wrong with respect to the employees' 30% share in the pre-existing ESOP. Not only did I spend a number of hours in the law library examining relevant deal points and IRS regulations on retirement plans under ERISA but I made my concerns known to my direct reporting relationship up the line. As the deal progressed management held to its position forcing a four dollar per share difference between the stock on the New York Stock Exchange and the $28 per share for the shares held by the employee predecessor ESOP. After attempts to get management's attention on the problem I decided to outline the problem in detail in a letter to senior management, the trustees of both ESOP trusts and the IRS cognizant office for the company. The financial effects on the predecessor ESOP trust and the employees holding stock interests in that ESOP were material in amount. In order to describe the existing problems with the deal, including the apparent conflict of interest that prevented the deal from being equitably executed, and avoid drawing attention to myself personally, I sent the letter unsigned to these different named individuals. My main objective was to get these principals to ascertain the nature of the conflicts, the impacts on company employees holding stock in the predecessor ESOP and to take action to correct the problem. As a result, ultimately the IRS who was required to approve the new ESOP plan refused to approve the plan because of this stock price differential between the two ESOP trusts. The IRS approved a plan, however, in which retiring employees would receive the $32 per share instead of $28 per share until such time as the price evaluated for the stock reached /exceeded $32 per share. This was an equitable outcome for the employees and therefore my objections were satisfied.

After this entire matter had been satisfied, I learned a lesson that when management takes a position and implements policy that is unfair or objectionable to the employees on reliable legal principles, give the company management a fair opportunity to rectify the problem first before you take any legal action.

The statements and comments in this Chapter reflect the author's opinion based on his observations but does not necessarily reflect the opinion of Parsons.

In 1990 a court on appeal threw out a lawsuit brought by disgruntled Parsons Employees who claimed that senior management, retirement committee and trustees of the ESOP committees violated their fiduciary duties to the employees when they executed a buyout of the outstanding shares and those in a predecessor ESOP. The court found that parsons senior management and retirement committee we're completely independent and exercised their fiduciary duties in accordance with the law. Notwithstanding this decision Parsons was required by the IRS in 1984/1985 to establish a prop price of $32 a share for all retirees of Parsons until such time as the valuated price for the shares reached/exceeded $32 per share. This was an equitable result for all employees under the revised and updated ESOP plan in 1985

How to survive in the corporation when responsible for making a controversial decision

In 1967 at the age of 26 I accepted an offer at Scripps Institution of Oceanography in La Jolla, California to be Director of contracts and procurement on the now famous Deep Sea Drilling Project (DSDP). Accepting this offer meant leaving the Chevron corporation land and legal division where I was in charge of department administration. For me, this job change and relocation was a significant promotional opportunity with a world-class organization to direct contracts and procurement activities of a multi- year project funded by the national science foundation, which was to become the most famous and ambitious inner space project of the Century. The DSDP was the brainchild of a group of scientists in scientific oceanographic institutions around the country named Joint Oceanographic Institutions for Deep Earth Sampling (JOIDES). Scripps Institution of Oceanography of the University of California, San Diego was the lead institution in the execution of

DSDP. My good friend Ken Brunot was the Manager of the DSDP and had previously spent numerous years at Chevron as a director of drilling operations for various oil plays. The objective of the DSDP was to demonstrate by deep sea drilling and coring in water depths of up to 20,000 feet that the continents were drifting in accordance with a hypothesis of a group of scientists who opposed the generally accepted theory that the earth's surface was in the arrangement of the present continents and had never changed over time. An opposing view by another body of scientists believed in continental drift, that is, that over time the continents had drifted apart and had rearranged into the current configuration on the maps. Therefore , DSDP was the brainchild of the latter group of scientists who were determined to discover the mechanisms and forces within the earth that could be attributed to a gigantic shift in landmasses over the years. This background sets up the context for a controversial decision which I made as Director of procurement and contracts. The drill ship Glomar Challenger would hold and transport refrigerated vans that would be the receptacles of core samples drilled on the ocean floor. The scientists on the project crafted a request for proposal to go out to a number of companies who were judged qualified to manufacture these vans and deliver them to the ship or other storage locations in good condition. Several well-known manufactures were named to be prospective bidders on the project.

There was one company in Sandusky, Ohio that was a small company but which nevertheless submitted the lowest bid for the vans by a significant sum. This was an opportunity to make a significant savings for the taxpayers/DSDP by buying the lowest bid vans. There was also a concern primarily by the scientists that this company would not be qualified to deliver the quality vans that the scientists desired. Therefore the scientists were reluctant to place the contract with the small firm from Sandusky. Determined to investigate the source of this bid I arranged for one of the scientific shipboard technicians to accompany me to Sandusky to do a source inspection of the plant and the management to determine if they appeared to be capable of meeting the requirements of the procurement standards. The two of us traveled in the dead of winter to Sandusky during a bitter snow storm. When we arrived in Sandusky we met up with a gentleman by the name of Zimmerman the owner and president of the company who took us on a tour of his plant. I was impressed by both Zimmerman and his plant which was clean and organized with a number of vans in progress in the manufacturing process. After a source inspection and an interview with Zimmerman I was convinced that this man and his operation would be capable of executing the procurement and deliver the needed vans to the project standards. The technician who accompanied me agreed. When we returned to DSDP headquarters we made the announcement that Zimmerman's company in Sandusky would receive the order at a substantial savings to the project and the taxpayers. When the order was prepared that would go to the contractor a provision was inserted in the contract that the vans would be delivered to the ship FOB destination. This meant that Zimmerman would be responsible for conveying the vans to the ultimate destination and that they must be received In good and workable condition in accordance with the contract standards. Nevertheless, much to my chagrin the vans were damaged in transit by train and were received in damaged condition. In spite of this my evaluation of Zimmerman had been accurate with respect to his character and responsibility for the services and the condition of the product he ultimately delivered. Zimmerman got on a plane in Ohio flew to Orange, Texas where the vans had been delivered and arranged to have every single one of them repaired and in order so they complied with the contract specifications. Never again during the course of the project did any of the vans fail to meet the requirements and specifications for refrigeration and retention of core samples. What I learned by this lesson was to follow your instincts and never hesitate to get a first-hand observation of the place where work is to be done and the character and responsibility of those who provide the execution and oversight of the work.

How to survive in the corporation where it is necessary to engage the support of an valued subordinate and establish a solid working relationship

It was 1977, I was age 36, and in charge contracts for the Power Division at Parsons in Pasadena, California. At this time corporate management reorganized and merged the larger Systems Division with the Power Division. The senior vice president of the power division, Bill Jack, was named to be the new senior vice president of the combined divisions which was called the Systems Division. Shortly after the merger was announced Bill Jack promoted me to manager of contracts for a much larger group of contracts administrators many of which were inherited from the Systems Division that was in charge of military contracts which were subject to the federal acquisition regulations (FAR) and the defense acquisition regulations (DAR). Government contracts required more contracts administrators because the special regulations adhered to in government procurement policy. I felt very comfortable with the FARs and DARs procurement policies because of my initial assignment in contracts at Aerojet- General Corporation where I learned government contracts that were subject to the federal acquisition regulations, therefore this was a natural adjustment for me to make at the time. I inherited a large staff of system division personnel who were assigned to the contracts group. Not all these people performed strictly contract work and would need to be reassigned to other parts of the company where they belong, or released.

There were several disgruntled senior contracts professionals in the contracts department who took exception to my being named the manager of contracts of the merged divisions. Ken was one of these individuals. Ken was a valuable employee assigned to one of the largest government contracts in the division. He was well liked by the manager of this large government contract and was relied on by the manager of the project to handle all contracts administration activities. However, the fact was that this project was not capturing enough profit on changes under the contract, while other aspects were being well handled and did not need to be changed. Ken initially resisted my ideas and recommendations for ways to handle his contract more effectively in achieving higher fees/profits. I tried to be straight forward with him in suggesting that adjustments had to be made when it came to changes being awarded under the contract, that were not currently being negotiated as fee/profit bearing . Ken still resisted after a month or two of the re-organization of contracts. Ken was a valuable employee who had learned contracts the hard way. He did not have a degree but nevertheless had become adept at his job. One day in the middle of a discussion with him, more of a debate, I said to Ken we are both Christians and we should be able to get along on that basis if nothing else and work together. The important thing was to find something in common around which we could relate and required a little humility on my part to find the common thread between us. From that moment on Ken and I had a terrific working relationship and he responded to my suggestions and ideas without hesitation. The lesson I learned was that as a manager it is sometimes necessary to humble yourself, and find a conciliatory common denominator in your relationship with an employee in order to make the relationship work. After a number of years in the position Ken and I enjoyed an outstanding relationship and continued to get along and I continued to appreciate his hard work and commitment to his project.

How to survive in the corporation by dealing with problem employees

In addition to the management responsibilities, I held as a manager of other people under me I learned that it was absolutely essential to deal with problem employees swiftly and decisively before they undermined the efforts of the organization or made serious and costly mistakes. At the age 45, in the time frame of 1986, I was appointed to an executive position, reporting to the President. The environmental subsidiary ultimately reached about 2000 employees. The organization was highly decentralized and geographically dispersed mostly in this country and with an office overseas. The organizational functions which I oversaw were information technology, accounting and finance, contracts, procurement, human resources, and arranging for the final review/approval of office leases around the country and the expenditure of major capital equipment utilized by the company in its activities. With a broad span of management and heavy workload a normal workday would usually last until about 7PM. In the fast-paced organization like this it was necessary that each manager carry his or her own load with minimum need for direct supervision and direction. The problem in which I learned a lesson arose from the contracts group in my organization. Ironically this dysfunction fell into an area where I had the most technical and managerial experience. It seemed that the problems both in performance and behavior arose from this work group exclusively. Importantly, I was remotely located from the problem area therefore was unable oversee the problem employees. The problem was limited to three senior contract administrators. One of them came from a major aerospace company where he was caught in a major layoff. The second employee was also a senior contract person with a legal background. The most senior of the group who reviewed most of the commercial contracts for the organization (i.e. non-federal) was also a legal graduate and handled a great deal the workload for the company. All three employees exhibited behavioral problems of one type or another. The contracts person from the aerospace company never truly adapted to the immediate environment. The second Senior contracts person who handled most of the federal contracts covered up a potentially serious contract error that needed fixing- a potential disciplinary situation. The third and most senior contracts person who handled a wide range of commercial and also some federal contracts was viewed as the most senior of the three although highly competent technically had a bad habit of verbally abusing his secretary. This had caused a couple of complaints to the President of the company by the secretary who was affected. Regardless of my counseling, this third contract administrator continued to verbally abuse his secretary. There was also a fourth senior contracts person assigned to the immediate office area who was in charge of procurement. This procurement manager was of character, knowledge and disposition where could step in and directly manage the three problem contracts administrators working in the same workspace nearby. At about this time I moved to a position in the parent corporation in charge of Special Projects. Before leaving, the first two senior contracts administrators left the company one went to a local engineering firm and the other one returned to the defense company who previously employed him. My next move at the environmental company would have been to put the procurement manager in direct charge of the three senior contracts people and promote him to the position of manager of contracts and procurement. I am confident this would've settled things down but did not have the chance to implement it before moving to a new position in the corporation. What I learned was that where a rotten immediate environment sets in more than one person can be affected. Where this occurs swift and decisive steps must be taken to rectify the environment of the problem personnel. I should have reacted more decisively and ended the problem quicker.

How to survive in the corporation by completing an important assignment on time and within budget

In 1964, age 23, after about one year working for the architect engineering division of Aerojet-General under the direction of contract manager Joe Eischen, Joe called to ask me to come to his office which I did promptly. Upon arriving at Joe's office he asked me to sit down that he had something to tell me. Apparently the company was engaged in a multi-year Air Force contract with a firm schedule delivery and firm fixed price. The contract was in trouble and needed to be brought back on schedule and within budget. A firm fixed price contract gives you little to no room to maneuver. If the contract is overrun the company loses money and it is still required to finish the job even though it runs out of money. The firm fixed price defines the level of financial compensation. Joe explained to me that the current contract was in trouble and that the project manager needed help but would not admit it. Joe indicated he was going to replace the current contract administrator for this project with me. He wanted me to get on top of things, get a quick pick up and then focus on getting the project back on schedule and within budget. He relieved the current Contract Administrator of his duties on the project and assigned me to take over. This was my first major assignment. The project was called the Closed Loop Telemetry Checkout System. It was to be installed at Vandenberg Air Force Base in Lompoc,California. The architect engineering division of Aerojet had the full responsibility for the turnkey installation, checkout and start- up of the system. The purpose of the system was to monitor the satellites being launched from Vandenberg Air Force Base. At the time I took over as contract administrator for the project many procured items were late delivery items and the project was over schedule and was over budget in terms of cost performance. After speaking to Joe it was determined that the most appropriate place for me to focus my efforts was expediting the procured items that would be incorporated into the system that were late in delivery to the company. I quickly pulled a procurement status report which showed all of the sub systems and components to be delivered, the name of the vendor and contact and the scheduled date of delivery for each item. The late delivery of many of these items was causing the project to slip schedule and go into a cost overrun situation. It was clear that my job had to be immediately performed and that I must promptly expedite each vendor delivery by discussing status on a frequent basis with the project managers who were at the vendor plants. As a result primarily of my efforts, subcontractor performance significantly improved and our project received the attention it needed. So the project got back on schedule and fabrication of the system improved significantly and the system was delivered to the site for installation on schedule. At the same time cost performance improved with the increased attention on schedule. Joe and I visited the site and inspected the system and the two of us got a good handle on where installation stood with the contractor who was doing it. We expedited that installation to the extent we were able and it was completed on time. When completed the system check out worked out smoothly and was accepted on time by the Air Force. In the end we made a 10% profit on the project and it was completed on schedule. After the project was completed and the profitability was measured, Joe submitted me for a promotional increase in pay and a promotion to the next level of contracts administration. This was my first opportunity to prove myself and it had been a success. What I learned was that the leading task on a project (in this case procurement) had to be identified immediately and then attention had to be given to these leading items promptly to assure that the project was completed on time and within budget.

How to survive in the corporation when communicating directly with the CEO/Chairman

To survive in the corporation it is important to restrict your communication on matters of personal performance to your direct line of reporting. You should only communicate directly with the chairman of the board or the CEO if the matter involved is one that would impact the overall corporation or is of significant social impact in which the company could be involved. In 1965, age 24, I was working for Chevron Corporation in the land and legal division. I was in charge of administrative activities for that division. For months I had been reading the text to speeches given by senior corporate executives and was impressed by the fact that there was never any mention in the speeches about environmental pollution and emission from fossil fuels and what the corporation might be doing to enhance the environment in this particular area. I decided that since this was a social matter that I would not have to communicate through my direct reporting line but could go directly to the chairman of the board/CEO with my concerns and expressed them straight to him. Of course, I sent a copy of my communication to the vice president of the land and legal division in San Francisco where the corporate headquarters was located as well to my immediate boss. And within a week I had received a response from the chairman/CEO thanking me for my thoughtful letter and advising me that he was directing the president of chevron research to send me a separate response in which she was going to outline the various programs going on in the corporation, in the research division, to deal with pollution from hydrocarbons. I received the second letter within several days of receiving the response from the chairman/CEO. I was informed by the land and legal division representative in San Francisco that the chairman of the board had asked for my file so he could review it before responding to my letter. The land and legal division representative in San Francisco told me that such correspondence should be routed through his office directly. I asked the representative if he would've passed this letter on my behalf and he said probably not. I told him that was the reason I sent the letter directly to the chairman/CEO and bypassed the land and legal division office in San Francisco. I learned an important lesson. But it was risky. Regardless of the content of the matter to bypass the direct line of reporting when communicating with the chairman of the board/ CEO of the company even though the chairman of the board/ CEO was gratified to receive your communication is a risky politically. Fortunately. in the succeeding years after that experience I continued to report matters of significance or pose questions of significance directly to the chairman and CEO when the matter fell outside the immediate scope of my job responsibilities. In the rest of my career I was never once criticized for directly communicating with the CEO/ chairman on a matter of significance to the corporation for example one that impacted the overall organization, it's resources, culture or structure. The lesson I learned was that it is always best to be bold and communicate with the chairman and CEO of the company when the matter was one of the significances that had an impact that would improve the overall corporation's image, structure, culture or profitability.

How to survive in the corporation by avoiding personal politics and focusing on corporate steering mechanisms

In charting your way through the corporation it is generally best to avoid your personal political views in your communications with others and to focus on the steering mechanisms of the business and where they are leading. By steering mechanisms I am referring to those activities and activity centers within the corporation such as marketing for example which must constantly be surveying the external environment for opportunities and threats and to ensure that the internal policies and processes and strategy of the company are on target with respect to the current environment in the external realm. On an ongoing basis corporate executives at all levels must connect themselves to the culture, resources and structure of the internal business operation to the external environmental threats and opportunities that exist. Once that connection is lost or misplaced the company tends to veer off track and move in the wrong direction. By way of example in the current environment of the 21st century corporations are tending to engage in political activities which have nothing to do with their core businesses. They tend to drift into such areas as Critical Race Theory spending and investing millions of dollars or large segments of their wealth in training people to think in a certain way about the political environment and in essence indoctrinate them in order to gain favor for a political administration that happens to be in power at any given time. By focusing on these political objectives the people of the organization, executive management and senior management focuses on issues which are entirely irrelevant to the important opportunities and threats that they face in the external environment. In other words these steering mechanisms lose alignment with realism in the marketplace and they find themselves sinking in utter despair. This is a much different strategy and practice than 20th century corporations used and is a far cry from what is necessary to remain successful in the marketplace today. Most usually the corporation becomes involved in such a downward spiraling strategy because it curries favor with the policies and values of the current political administration in Washington DC. Senior management who directs the firm and leads it in this direction is making a sad mistake and will soon find themselves in utter despair and in a blind alley wishing they had kept alignment between their internal and external environments. Typically the internal environment of the Corporation consists of its structure or the way it is organized, its culture in other words it's values and beliefs and thirdly it's resources which involves its principal prime technologies and abilities.

How to survive in the corporation in the face of the career setback

It was 1996, age 55, and I was manager of corporate services reporting to the president of Parsons engineering science a wholly-owned subsidiary of Parsons Corporation. In this position I had the responsibility to oversee information technology, accounting and finance, contracts, procurement, and human resources in addition to reviewing and handling approvals for both office leases around the company and capital equipment expenditures. It was a high visibility position reporting to the president of the company. At any time I had approximately 50 employees reporting up through the different activities reporting to me at the corporate office.

In 1996 the parent corporation decided to merge Parsons engineering science into an existing Parsons entity known as the Systems and infrastructure division. In many ways this was the reverse of what happened to me in the earlier stages of my career when the power division which I was a part was merged with the systems division when my then mentor and boss Bill Jack was named to take over the newly combined divisions in which he appointed me manager of contracts. Only the reverse was happening now and I was being merged into a division of the company and a new president and CEO with whom I was not familiar who had been named the leader in the new organization as merged. This new leader of the combined organizations already had his people lined up to take over in the new organization. It was quite possible I would not be in the picture for a new slot at the level I had in Parsons Engineering Science.

Nevertheless I cooperated fully in the transition process in which I transferred each of my organizations seamlessly into the new organization activity by activity, person by person. The present CEO of the newly merged company was pleased with my support in carrying out this transition smoothly and cooperatively. He told me that. Nevertheless right after Christmas in 1996 the new president called me into his office, closed the door and gave me the news that there was not a position in the new company that matched my previous job and that if I agreed I could remain with the company in Contracts which was the area I started in back in 1976 and which I had managed for a number of years. Although I was disappointed because I would take a salary cut in the move I told the new president that I felt that this was a new challenge that I had to confront and I agreed to remain with the company at that moment. I would be reporting back to contracts, a field which I loved and was good in, and would be reporting to longtime friend Jess Harmon who I had helped in the early stages of his career move up the ladder and eventually take over the position that I had occupied. The presence of karma could not be stronger than at this time in my career. Nevertheless after interviewing with another large engineering company in the same city, I did my math and determined to remain with the newly merged company as a principal contracts person performing special projects that were challenging and complex within the division as newly merged. The Director of Contracts & Procurement who I reported to, being very good friends, never had any problems in working together and within two years I had received promotions and increases which restored my compensation to the level it was when I joined the newly merged company contracts group in 1996. In addition, and because I did not move to another firm, my Employee Stock Ownership Plan compensation continued to generate stock allocations to my account. In addition to my work responsibilities in my previous position at Parsons engineering science(Parsons ES), I had received my MBA degree in 1993 while still an employee of Parsons ES. At the time of my transfer to the newly merged company and into my present position I was continuing to work on the second Masters Degree at

Claremont Graduate University at the Drucker School and would soon complete that degree as well. I found a tremendous amount of challenge and excitement in my educational advancements while with the company although I can't honestly say that in terms of pay these additional degrees probably only had less than a profound impact on my compensation. Nevertheless at this point in my career I found a tremendous challenge and enjoyment of continuing my education and completed a second Master of Science degree in advanced management in 1998. At this time I was only two years from when I would actually retire in the year 2000 at age 59. During the ensuing years I have retained some contacts with Parsons which have been helpful to me in advancing my writing career. What I learned during the latter years of my career was that career setbacks are possible but can be overcome by perseverance and a steadfastness to climb back up the ladder and then end on a positive note on the last day of work. In retrospect that's how I feel today about my career at Parsons, and the other entities in which I was fortunate enough to serve and grow over the years.

How to survive in the corporation when a problem employee needs to be terminated

In 1998, age 58, I inherited a problem employee when I took over as manager of Parsons infrastructure Contracts. Mary was a lawyer who had graduated from the one of the top law schools in Southern California. She was also a minority employee. Mary had the undesirable behavior of reporting to work significantly late most mornings. She stated she was out at night frequently salsa dancing and socializing. In accordance with our human resource policies I counseled her on her behavior told her that this reporting late must end. Nevertheless the behavior of late reporting continued and showed no signs of ending. She was counseled again in accordance with human resource policy about chronic late reporting to work and told her it could lead to her termination. Since her behavior continued to report late to work there was one or two courses available for addressing the problem. First, she could be terminated for cause after progressive counseling sessions in accordance with Parsons policy.. Second she could be laid off in a reduction in work force and terminated. In the past week I identified a contract administrator in the group whose work had slackened due to completed work assignments who had available time to absorb additional workload.

Accordingly I called a meeting with my boss the vice president of contracts to sit down in a meeting between the three of us to notify her that she was being laid off due to a reduction in department workload. When we met in the vice president's office I informed her that she was being terminated by layoff for a reduction of workload. This avoided the need to terminate her for cause due to the late reporting but accomplished the same objective which was to eliminate her from the Contracts group without further delay.

When I notified her that she was no longer needed and was being laid off she seemed taken by surprise that there was no job available in my group for her. I then excused myself got up and left the room leaving she and the vice president together. When Mary returned to her office moments later I had my secretary help her empty Mary's office and walk her out to her car. Later my secretary informed me that Mary said she deserved to be laid off based on her behavior. There was never any legal issues raised with regard to her termination and we never heard anything further from Mary about her termination. What I learned from this experience is it there is always more than one way to achieve an objective in this particular case it was more expedient and effective to select a layoff for Mary rather than terminate her for cause. It also spared Mary's employment record since a layoff is more acceptable than a termination for cause. Hopefully Mary was able to correct her tardiness and find a job after the layoff.

How to survive in the corporation by researching the capabilities/capacity of your clients

Sometime in 1965, age 24, while working for standard oil company of California in La Habra California (hereinafter Chevron) I became acquainted with a scientist who worked for Chevron Research. This scientist ran an x-ray Diffractometer system for Chevron Research Lab. The scientist was going to be leaving Chevron research soon to go to work at the University of California Riverside where he would head up a geothermal resources program that would focus on the Imperial Valley of California. For purposes of reference we will call the scientist Dr. Heatrock(hereafter "DR") The DR lined up grant and other funding sources to support his work in the geothermal area in imperial Valley and other places. DR. also equipped his laboratory in Riverside with an x-ray diffractometer system to continue his work and services in mineralogy studies for other clients of his lab. One of these clients, a major source of business, was the deep sea drilling project at Scripps institution of oceanography in La Jolla California. DR held degrees from prestigious universities and was generally seen as a very bright scientist. His primary funding sources at the University would be for geothermal exploration in the imperial Valley of California and a revenue stream from his laboratory system in which he would examine core samples for mineralogy content and characteristics. DR had ambitions to form a national geothermal resources /consortium program at the University similar in concept to the highly successful Deep Sea Drilling Project at Scripps Institution of Oceanography in La Jolla California. After serving five years on the deep sea drilling project I was ready to move on to the next major challenge. In response to discussions with DR., he offered me a position as an Administrator in the geothermal resources program at the University of California Riverside which I accepted. During his tenure at UC Riverside or at some point, DR. acquired an interest in pursuing limited partnership operations in the Imperial Valley for geothermal commercial investigation. I was not aware of this at the time until he disclosed it after about one year of employment at UC Riverside. A complicating factor was that DR's funding sources appeared to be drying up at the University of California Riverside and he also decided to move on and set up his own business in the geothermal resources area in the commercial sector, developing those resources for commercial use. In any event the DR left the University and commenced business operations in his new geothermal business. To complicate in the weeks before he left DR had invited numerous world-class geologists from leading institutions to the University in Riverside for a tour of the geothermal resources and numerous presentations about the resource of the imperial Valley including flying the University plane over the geothermal fields to get an aerial view of them. Shortly afterwards, and before he left the University, he divulged to me his plan for limited partnership operations in the geothermal field and that he was going to leave the University. I expressed surprise.

Promptly afterwards, I obtained a position at General Atomic Company in San Diego where I spent the next five years in contracts until 1976 when I joined the Power Division at Parsons (a global engineering business in Pasadena, California) as a contacts specialist. A few months later I was notified by Bill Jack, the manager of the Power Division that the DR. would be visiting for a meeting in which Parsons was to be requested to perform services in connection with DR's operations in the Imperial Valley. When I informed the division manager that I had extensive dealings in the past with DR and informed of the possible performance problems that could arise in dealing with him, the division manager requested that I sit in on the meeting. When the Meeting took place the DR requested Parsons undertake an engineering project for one of his power plants in the Imperial Valley. After a short sidebar meeting between Bill Jack, the manager of business development Parsons and myself it was decided that Parsons would prepare the designs as requested but would require advance payments be made to ensure that revenue under the project was always matched or exceeded Parsons expenses. DR agreed to the advance payment clause which was incorporated into the contract and the work was performed and payments made in advance and the work was successfully completed.

Fast forward about three years while I was in a different position as Parsons manager of contracts, the executive vice president for development at Parsons initiated independently discussions with the DR regarding the completion of engineering and the construction oversight of the geothermal plant in the Imperial Valley. Commitments were made by Parsons under a loan guarantee with the Department of Energy for this project. In retrospect neither the executive vice president for development nor apparently any other senior executive researched to determine whether there was information within the organization that would've informed them to the problems that could potentially be encountered in conducting business with DR. The Executive Vice President nor any other member of senior management apparently consulted anyone that was close to the previous project to determine that doing business with DR could be highly problematic. An entirely separate team of engineers and other personnel for Parsons was assembled to perform the new work. No advance payment clause was negotiated to ensure that Parsons received compensation for the work on time. As a consequence the project fell into trouble both schedule and financial wise and had to be brought to an end, an early termination in which Parsons experienced some losses for its efforts.

What I learned from this experience was that unless senior management who makes commitments for new work researches the organization to determine information about the client's past record of performance that serious problems can be encountered that are costly to the company. Typically Senior management should be the ones who initiate such a research within the organization to determine capacity and capability of a client.. Too frequently out of an abundance of excitement and desire for new work, people in a sales position will sometimes fail to consider the downside of the new project or overlook to place safeguards in the contract and the relationship that ensures that payments will be sufficient to cover expenditures at any given time, and that the financial capacity and experience of the client are suitable for engaging a contract relationship.

AFTERWORD

The purpose of this book is to inform those in corporate life, or who may be ready to join it, of the personal experiences which taught me something special about surviving in the corporation and its sometimes jungle- like environment. The book will lead the reader through the initial and final stages of one person's career. Along the corporate trail a sudden turn can result in either a major gain or loss in one's corporate fortunes. Surviving the Corporation is the individual experience and outcome for each person who takes up the shield of corporate life as a career. Since my career ended in the year 2000, life has mainly been good to me and I have been able to feed off 40 years of corporate existence by publishing several books based on a lifetime of experiences, or based on political events that have shaped our times. Corporate afterlife for me has been one of travel to such places as China, Canada, Tasmania, Australia, New Zealand and the western and southern areas of the US. I have enjoyed a busy existence which has included both publishing six books including this one, and consulting on my favorite subject of contract administration, and on the subject of employee stock ownership as a corporate strategic device. The books I have written include the political analyses in A view from the Eagle's Nest, when justice failed, an assessment of the Obama era. There is also the book titled Discovering your boundaries – living within yourself, which is a self-help/personal development book which focuses on lessons learned within my life time that I pass on to the reader for consideration and improvement in their life. I also write about my son Chris in the book A life in darkness – the drug addicted child, in which the reader and I come to grips with living the life of the parent of a drug addicted child and then recovering from the death of that child through a tragic accident. In addition to the book on surviving in the Corporation – The employee handbook, other business and finance related book by the author include Contract administration pitfalls and solutions for architect engineer projects, which condenses in 40 pages a complex subject made simple to understand by the author. The final book, in addition to this one, is titled Increasing firm competitive advantage through the use of an employee stock ownership plan (ESOP) which is a book about the strategic uses of employee retirement plans using an ESOP trust which enhances the work environment, motivates employees to merge their interests with the corporate interests and to provide for a substantial retirement benefit for long-term/committed workers. In essence this is a about worker capitalism and strategic corporate benefits of an ESOP company.

After more than 40 years of corporate life and more than 20 years of retirement I continue to feed generously from my corporate experiences in my corporate afterlife as an author and consultant. I also continue to enjoy a number of personal friends who once worked with me in the Corporation life that I led.

I hope that this book about Surviving in the Corporation will enhance and enrich your life and success in the Corporation.

www.ingramcontent.com/pod-product-compliance
Ingram Content Group UK Ltd.
Pitfield, Milton Keynes, MK11 3LW, UK
UKHW022209230426
12048UKWH00016BA/728